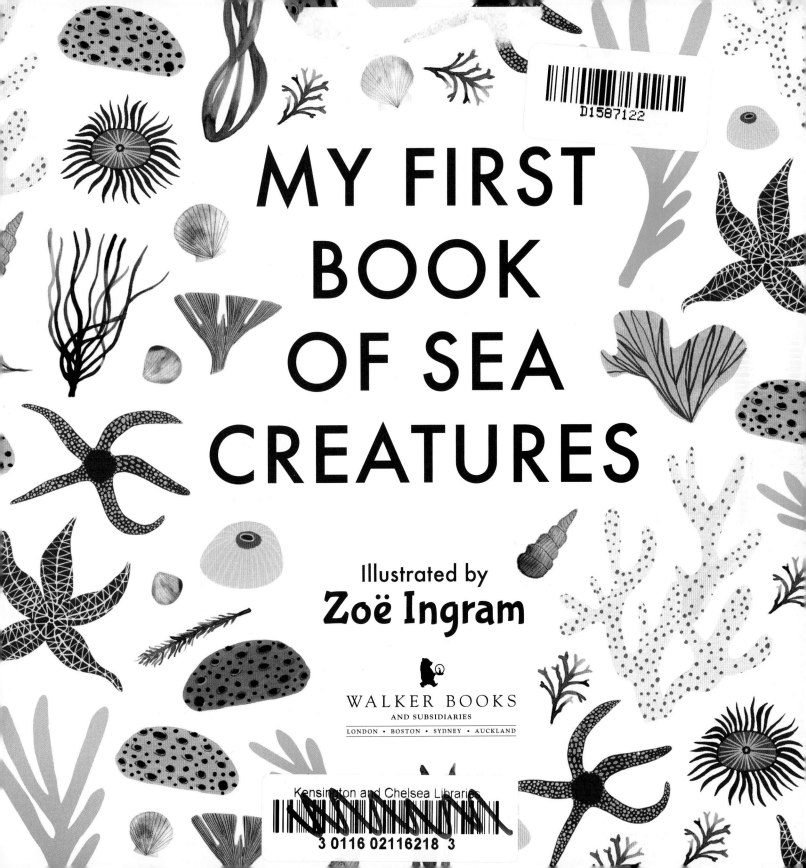

MY FIRST BOOK OF SEA CREATURES

Illustrated by
Zoë Ingram

WALKER BOOKS
AND SUBSIDIARIES
LONDON · BOSTON · SYDNEY · AUCKLAND

Clownfish

There are nearly 30 known species of clownfish. Most are the recognizable orange and white, but some are black and white. They make their homes among the stinging tentacles of anemones, to protect themselves from prey.

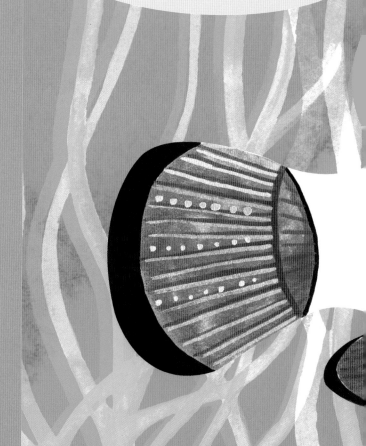

Size

11 cm

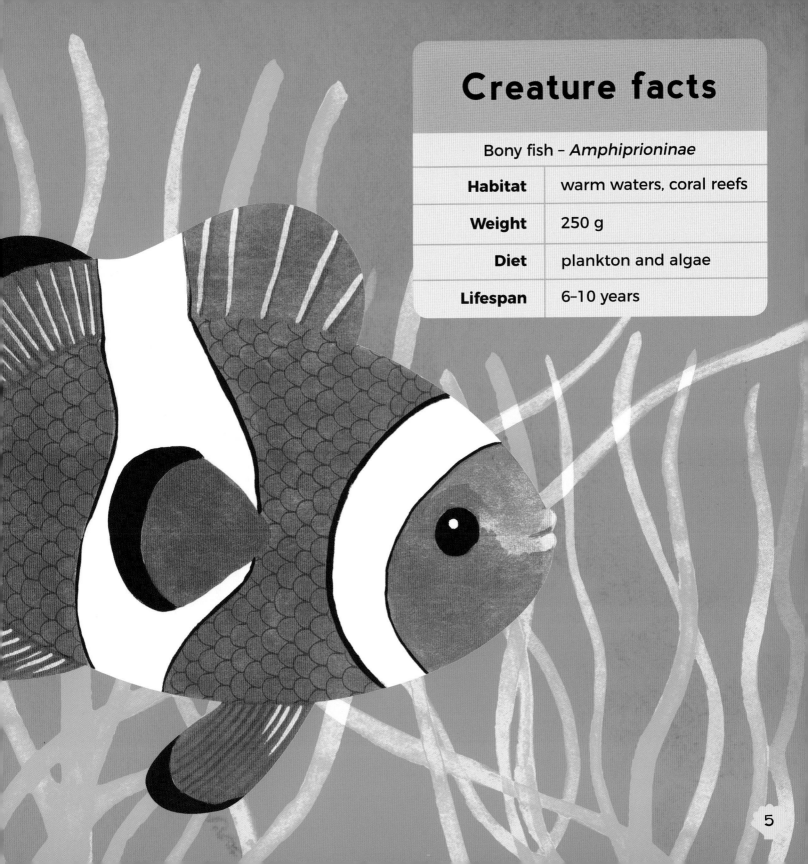

Creature facts

Bony fish – *Amphiprioninae*	
Habitat	warm waters, coral reefs
Weight	250 g
Diet	plankton and algae
Lifespan	6–10 years

Did you know?
Manta rays can jump completely out of the water. No one knows exactly why they do this!

Creature facts

Cartilaginous fish – *Manta birostris*

Habitat	tropical and subtropical waters
Weight	over 1 t
Diet	plankton and fish
Lifespan	50 years

Giant manta ray

These graceful creatures are one of the largest types of fish in the world. They are intelligent animals with acute senses of sight and smell and have very large brains. They give birth to a single pup every two or three years.

Size

up to 9 m wide

Moon jellyfish

Jellyfish have lived on Earth for millions of years. They are made mostly of water and have no brain, blood, heart or eyes. Moon jellies have short tentacles and are easily recognized by the four horseshoe shapes on their bell.

Size

5–40 cm

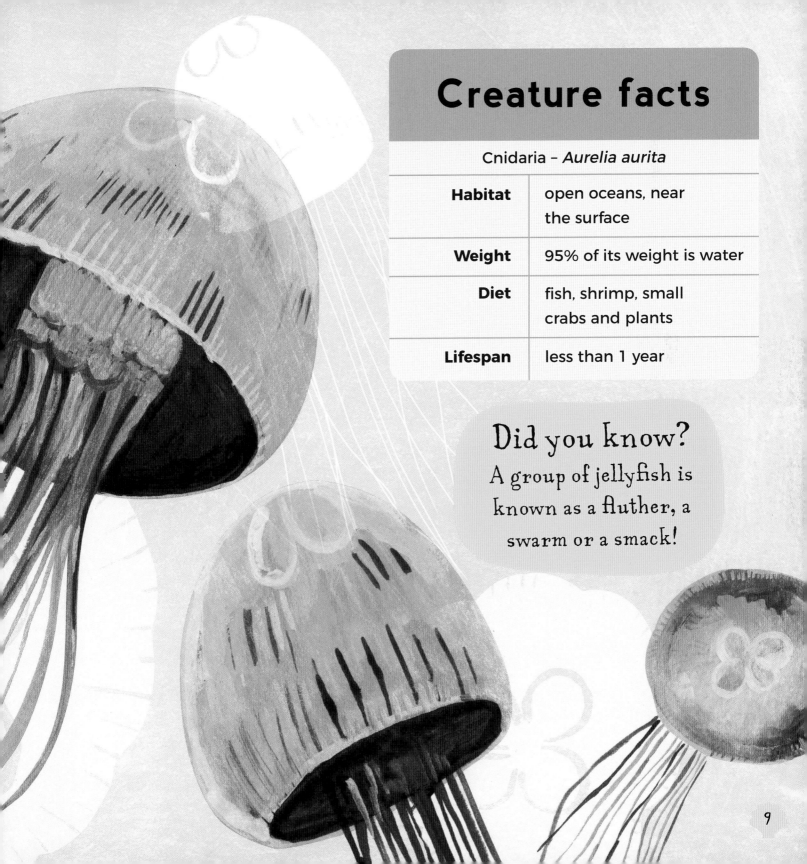

Creature facts

Cnidaria – *Aurelia aurita*	
Habitat	open oceans, near the surface
Weight	95% of its weight is water
Diet	fish, shrimp, small crabs and plants
Lifespan	less than 1 year

Did you know?

A group of jellyfish is known as a fluther, a swarm or a smack!

Creature facts

Crustacean – *Paguroidea*

Habitat	coastal waters
Weight	200–500 g
Diet	plankton, fish, algae and invertebrates
Lifespan	about 10 years

Hermit crab

Unlike true crabs, hermit crabs do not have a hard shell and have to make their homes in the empty shells of other animals. As they grow, they need to find a bigger shell to move into.

Did you know?
Hermit crabs are always right-handed.

Size
up to 10 cm

11

Starfish

Starfish (also known as sea stars) aren't actually fish – they're invertebrates. There are about 2,000 different types and they come in lots of different colours. They usually have five arms and they can regrow a limb if they lose one.

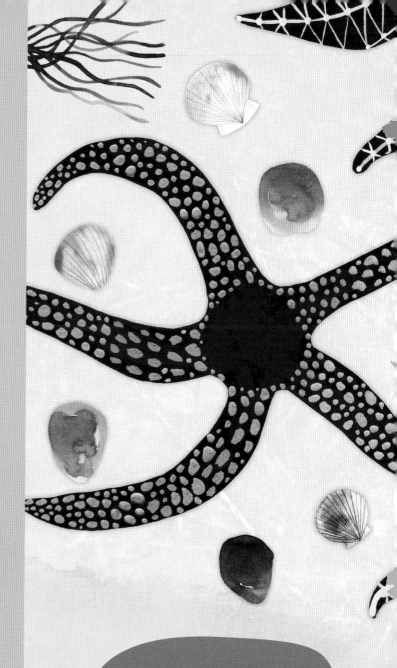

Size

10–30 cm

Did you know?
Starfish don't have blood or brains.

Creature facts

Echinoderm – *Asteroidea*

Habitat	rock pools, coral reefs and kelp beds
Weight	up to 5 kg
Diet	clams, oysters and snails
Lifespan	up to 35 years

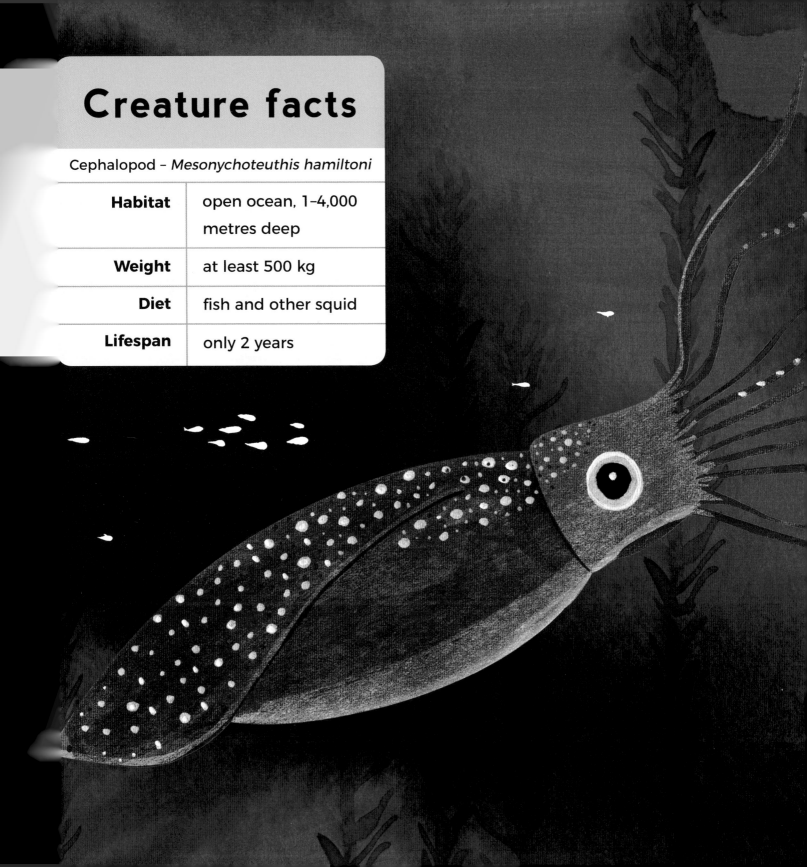

Creature facts

Cephalopod – *Mesonychoteuthis hamiltoni*	
Habitat	open ocean, 1–4,000 metres deep
Weight	at least 500 kg
Diet	fish and other squid
Lifespan	only 2 years

Colossal squid

The colossal squid is the largest invertebrate in the world and has the largest eyes of any living creature – they're the size of dinner plates. They have eight arms and two longer tentacles covered with suckers and sharp hooks for catching prey.

Did you know?
Despite their size, colossal squid only need to eat 30 grams of food a day.

Size

14 m

Narwhal

Known as the unicorn of the sea, the male narwhal grows a tusk up to three metres long. The tusk is actually a tooth that grows through their top lip in a left-handed spiral. Their numbers are under threat from climate change and pollution.

Size

4–5.5 m
(excluding tusk)

Did you know?

A narwhal can dive down to over 1,500 metres.

Creature facts

Mammal – *Monodon monoceros*

Habitat	subpolar and polar waters
Weight	up to 1.6 t
Diet	fish, shrimp and squid
Lifespan	30–40 years

Creature facts

Cnidaria – *Anthozoa*	
Habitat	warm, clear, shallow water
Weight	same density as sand
Diet	algae and plankton
Lifespan	hundreds of years

Did you know?
The Great Barrier Reef is so large it can be seen from space.

Coral

Coral look like plants, but are actually small stationary animals called polyps. They live in groups, growing an outside shell which then becomes coral. Over thousands of years, if lots of coral grow together, they create a reef – an important habitat for fish.

Size
up to 30 cm

Great white shark

Sharks are the largest predators of the seas. They have 300 sharp triangular teeth, lined up in seven rows, so if one drops out there's always another one ready to take its place. They can swim at 60 kph and travel huge distances. Unlike most sharks, great whites are partially warm-blooded.

Size

4.6–6 m

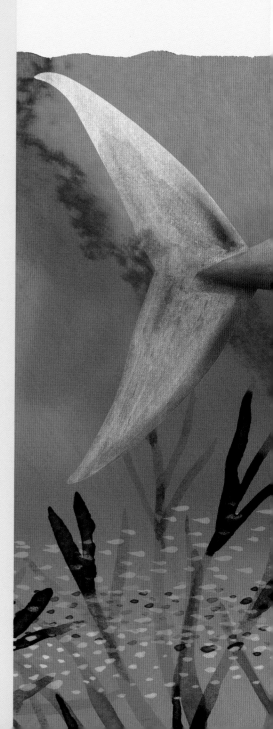

Did you know?
A shark can smell a single drop of blood in 100 litres of water.

Creature facts

Cartilaginous fish – *Carcharodon carcharias*

Habitat	cooler coastal waters
Weight	2.5 t or more
Diet	fish, rays, seals, sea lions and small whales
Lifespan	up to 70 years

Creature facts

Bony fish – *Tetraodontidae*	
Habitat	tropical and subtropical waters
Weight	up to 13 kg
Diet	invertebrates and algae
Lifespan	about 10 years

Did you know?
Pufferfish are surprisingly
poor swimmers!

Pufferfish

There are over 120 different types of pufferfish. When they are threatened, they fill themselves with water, pushing out their spikes and puffing up into a big ball to scare predators away. They are very poisonous, but are considered a delicacy in some parts of the world.

Size

17–60 cm

Harbour seal

Harbour seals live in large groups and communicate mostly underwater. They are shy but curious creatures who are known for their intelligence. The female has one pup each year which will be able to swim from birth.

Size

1.2–1.8 m

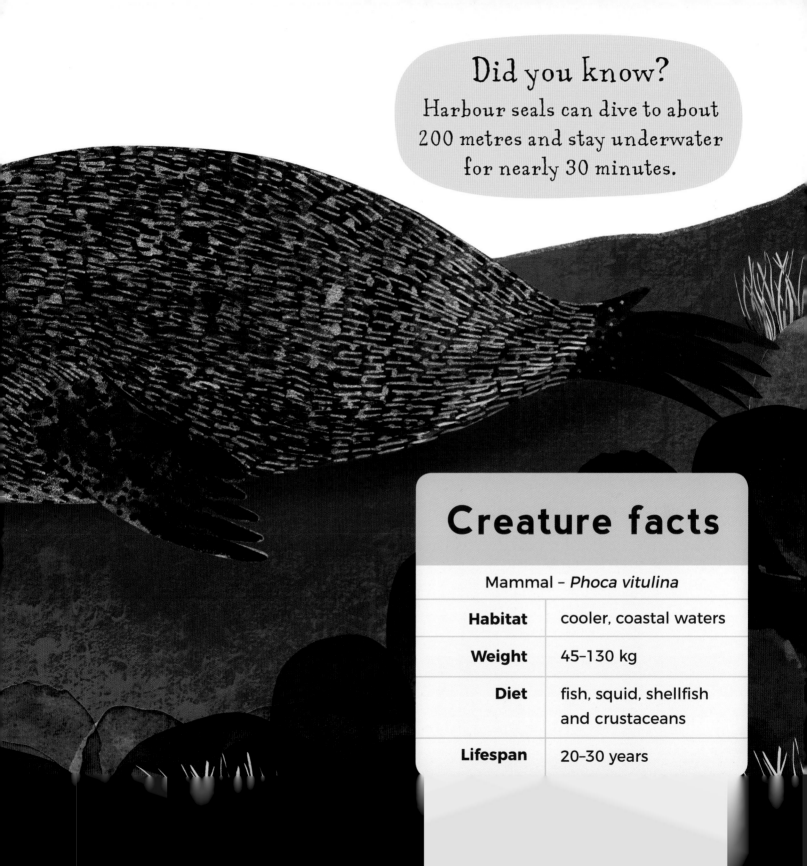

Did you know?
Harbour seals can dive to about 200 metres and stay underwater for nearly 30 minutes.

Creature facts

Mammal – *Phoca vitulina*	
Habitat	cooler, coastal waters
Weight	45–130 kg
Diet	fish, squid, shellfish and crustaceans
Lifespan	20–30 years

Creature facts

Bony fish – *Lophiiformes*	
Habitat	deep sea
Weight	up to 50 kg
Diet	anything they can get their teeth into!
Lifespan	unknown (thought to be at least 3 years)

Did you know?
The glow is created by bioluminescent bacteria that live inside the anglerfish's lure.

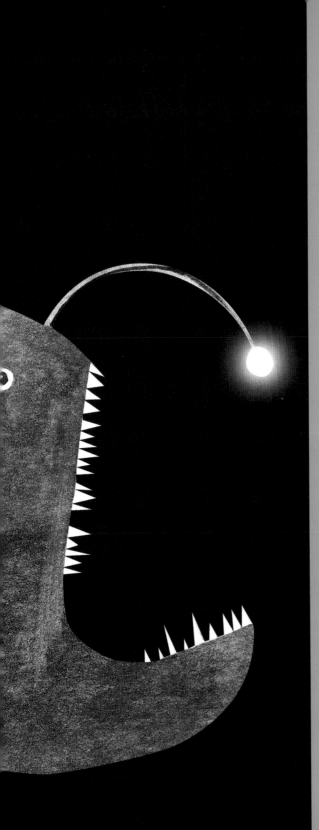

Anglerfish

Anglerfish live deep in the ocean – at least two kilometres down. The female has a lure that lights up to attract prey. It looks like a fishing rod which gives them their name. The female is much larger than the male.

Size
20–100 cm

Seahorse

Seahorses' heads are shaped like a horse's and they use their curly tails to hold onto plants so that they don't get swept away. Seahorses can camouflage themselves to hide from predators. There are about 40 different types of seahorse.

Size

17–30 cm

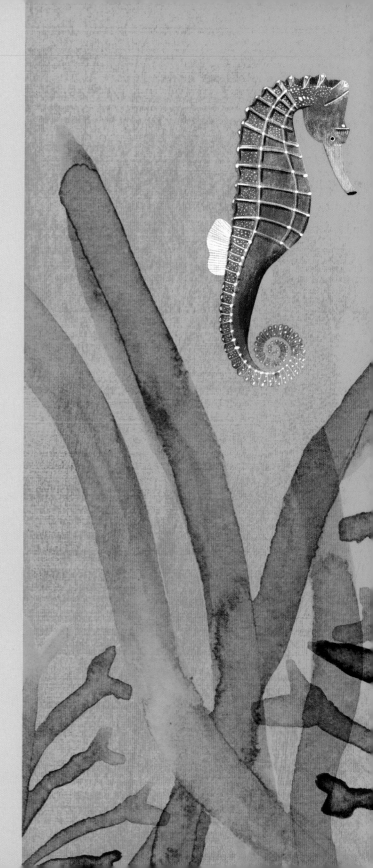

Creature facts

Bony fish – *Hippocampus kuda*	
Habitat	warmer coastal waters
Weight	up to 200 g
Diet	small crustaceans
Lifespan	3 years

Did you know?
The male seahorse looks
after the eggs until they
are ready to hatch.

Creature facts

Mammal – *Tursiops truncatus*

Habitat	warm oceans and coastal waters
Weight	500–650 kg
Diet	small fish, shrimp and squid
Lifespan	40–50 years

Did you know?
Dolphins have to surface to breathe but can hold their breath underwater for seven minutes.

Bottlenose dolphin

One of the most loved animals in the world, dolphins are highly intelligent. They are experts at communication and use clicks, squeaks and whistles to talk. They can swim at speeds of over 30 kph and travel in groups called pods.

Size

up to 4 m

Green sea turtle

These gentle giants travel long distances between where they feed and where they lay their eggs. The females dig nests in sandy beaches and lay clutches of about 100–200 eggs. They hatch after two months and the baby turtles must rush to the sea before they get eaten.

Size

up to 1.5 m

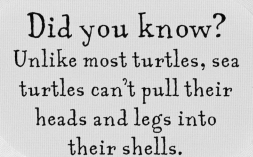

Did you know?
Unlike most turtles, sea turtles can't pull their heads and legs into their shells.

Creature facts

Reptile – *Chelonia mydas*

Habitat	warm coastal waters
Weight	65–130 kg
Diet	seagrass and algae
Lifespan	up to 80 years

Creature facts

Reptile – *Laticauda colubrina*

Habitat	warm and tropical coastal waters
Weight	up to 1.8 kg
Diet	eels and small fish
Lifespan	10 years

Did you know?
Sea snakes can swallow prey larger than themselves!

34

Sea snake

The banded sea snake lives in coral reefs in the eastern Indian and western Pacific Oceans. They spend more time on land than in the water but can dive for 30 minutes before they have to come back up for air. They are very venomous and paralyze their prey before they swallow them whole.

Size
75–128 cm

Octopus

Octopuses have eight arms and if one gets cut off, they can re-grow it. They have no bones, so they can hide in really small spaces to escape from predators. They can also change colour for camouflage. If they are discovered, they squirt black ink to hide themselves in, then make a quick getaway.

Size

30–100 cm

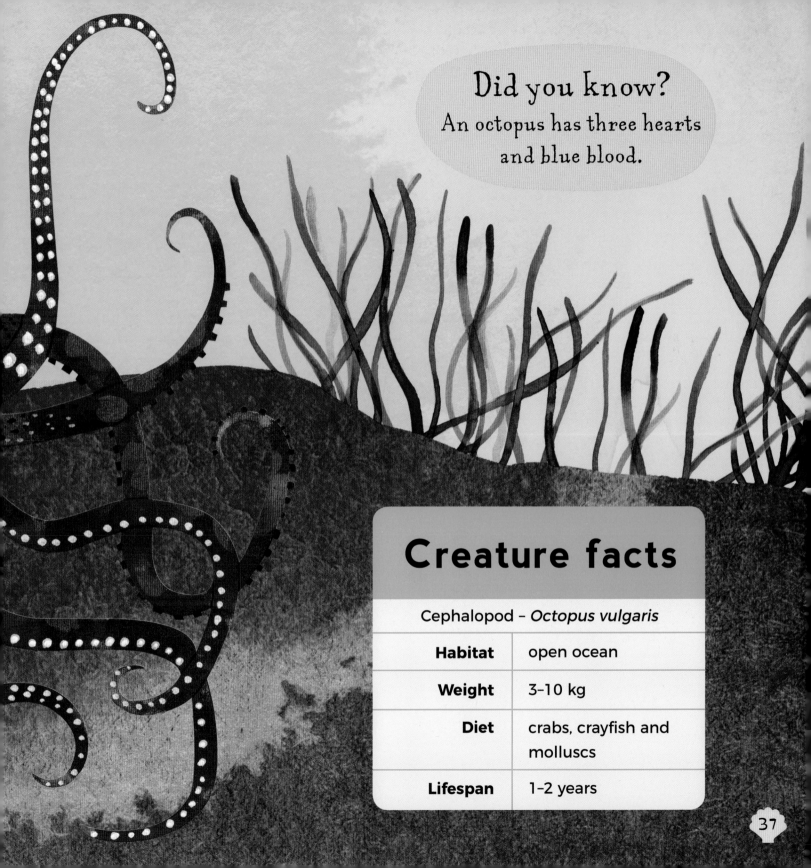

Did you know?
An octopus has three hearts and blue blood.

Creature facts

Cephalopod – *Octopus vulgaris*	
Habitat	open ocean
Weight	3–10 kg
Diet	crabs, crayfish and molluscs
Lifespan	1–2 years

Creature facts

Mammal – *Enhydra lutris*

Habitat	rocky shores and kelp forests of the Pacific Ocean
Weight	up to 45 kg
Diet	sea urchins, crabs, clams and snails
Lifespan	females up to 20 years, males up to 15 years

Did you know?
Sea otters rest their food on their tummies – just like plates – when they eat!

Sea otter

Sea otters have incredibly thick fur (140,000 hairs per square centimetre!) which keeps them warm in cold water. They spend their whole lives in the water and sleep floating on their backs, holding paws so that they don't float away from their group.

Size

up to 1.5 m

Shrimp

Shrimp live all over the world and there are over 2,000 varieties. Common shrimp have ten legs and long antennae. They are very strong swimmers and propel themselves backwards. Larger shrimp can live as deep as 5,000 metres.

Size

up to 8 cm

Creature facts

Crustacean – *Crangon crangon*	
Habitat	everywhere
Weight	about 4 g
Diet	algae and plankton
Lifespan	up to 3 years

Did you know?
A single shrimp can lay
up to a million eggs
in one go.

Creature facts

Mammal – *Balaenoptera musculus*

Habitat	everywhere apart from the Arctic
Weight	190 t
Diet	krill
Lifespan	80–90 years

Did you know?
Their tongue can weigh
the same as an elephant.

Blue whale

The largest animal ever to have lived on earth, these magnificent mammals live in small groups called pods. They eat tiny creatures called krill – up to 40 million a day. A baby blue whale (calf) is eight metres long and already weighs over three tons.

Size

30 m

Index

Tick off the animals that you have seen in the sea.

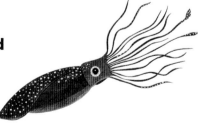

○ **Hermit crab**

Page 10

○ **Moon jellyfish**

Page 8

○ **Narwhal**

Page 16

○ **Octopus**

Page 36

○ **Pufferfish**

Page 22

○ **Seahorse**

Page 28

○ **Sea otter**

Page 38

○ **Sea snake**

Page 34

○ **Shrimp**

Page 40

○ **Starfish**

Page 12

**For my deep sea, octopus-loving diver.
I hope that we get to see at least some of
these amazing creatures together someday.
And Toby.**

First published 2021 by Walker Books Ltd
87 Vauxhall Walk, London SE11 5HJ

2 4 6 8 10 9 7 5 3 1

This book has been typeset in Futura,
Montserrat, Nevis and Aunt Mildred

Printed in China

British Library Cataloguing in Publication Data:
a catalogue record for this book is available
from the British Library

ISBN 978-1-4063-9492-4

www.walker.co.uk